That Little Thing Called
LIFE

A Collection of Poems
By

Ted W. Farcasin

Tai da Press
Hesperia, CA

Author: Farcasin, Ted W.
Printed in: United States of America, 2011

Library of Congress Control Number: 2011931319

ISBN: 978-0-615-49761-7

Table of Contents

Preface

Poetry is the pithy expression of intellectual, emotional and spiritual truth. It springs forth from an inspired heart and touches all aspects of the human experience. It does not make claims of flawlessness, marketability or profound clarity. In fact, in many instances the opposite is often true. Robert Browning was criticized for his obscurity and arduous nature of poetic expression. Simultaneously, he was lauded for his versatility and fecundity. Effectually, he did the very thing that people of his rank and genre do – as an artist he produced art. Poetry then does not place on the poet the requirements of external realities such as pretense, position or self-abasement. Rather, it is a matter of a compelling mind, will and emotion that seeks to make meaning in the world. Perhaps, as you read the writings herein your own "state of being" will be enriched and eyes cast heavenward

Ted W. Farcasin

For those who love to behold.

Recovery

Recovery runs a continuous course.
Not hindered by passion or subtle remorse
Stained by distress, tempered by tumult and lashed by lies
The heart of the righteous rejoices with muted replies.
Now, can the ebb of life defy what God has begun?
Can any pluck out or is faith undone?
Is tenderness or grace removed from those who want?
Does the agony of stripping leave bitterness to haunt?
Certain things will always be; like wind, water and stone.
Beyond the spoken, progressive revelation a hallowed moan.
The purity of future travail evokes a sanctified groan.
Confident Christ is perfecting in movement or peace.
Deepening and plowing an everlasting spiritual crease

Personal Reflections

_____

_____

_____

_____

_____

1

First Born

Knocking at the sinews of life that was my firstborn
Heard I, this solace that was coming into the world.
Of course, not traditionally, Caesar was his moniker.
Color indescribable was this breath of life.
Eyes of my soul illumined joy, heart cried son.
He carried something of me, something of God.
Thoughts none, thought's grand, as he rose to living.
This child puts to past the sudden, the lost or the last.
Strain daily does he to lift the tips of icebergs off of me.
Smiles so sublime they magically pinpoint the heart.
Bridged by vision the conscious hope of an aligned path
So sets dream and hand to grasp a fate yet to be.
Sidle up to shadows in hollow-lonely repose did I.
Life has arrived as only the great creator knows.

Personal Reflections

_____

_____

_____

_____

_____

2

Friends – Close

Here is where the ineffable is untouched.
Faint only, the glimmer of pretense.
Long are the limbs that grasp at the heart.
Short on the snipes that fracture relationships
Determined on your life worth living
Scarred at joints joined, bone calls to bone
Moored with you beneath the burden
Refrain; do their lips the passage of scorn.
Bury they do, your thoughts of demise.
With sweetened mercy they raise your being.
With pierced truth they restore your mettle.
They'll see you in the shadows.
Incumbent on you is the press of the link.
You know their names, they remain, friends - close.

Personal Reflections

_____

_____

_____

_____

_____

Gentleness

Soothing and kindly lay down on this pillow
Calm comes in with the goodness of joy.
Why not lean on this staff and prolong days.
So nice, so clean, so unreserved is this nod
Play along in leniency and there remain.
See with the eyes of fragrant tolerance.
Step aside from the coarse rebuff
Look again at the hand that warmed the wound.
Walk kindly with the one that walked humbly.
Lean lightly on the one that winks eternally.
If bliss is lost in the morass of confusion then
tides are turned with the gentleness of touch.
Softly is a word spoken that stills the anger.
So, attractive this Spiritual fruit gentleness.

Personal Reflections

_____

_____

_____

_____

_____

Heartache

Why does it have to hurt so much?
It doesn't hurt so much it hurts immensely.
It pierces the soul, it bangs your bones, and anguish riles the being.
Organs play songs of remorse they shrivel with this malaise.
This bolt cracks even those who are stony pillars.
No vagabond can eschew this stealthy stalker.
Its footprints pervade garden parties even where frivolity reigns.
Weeping faces cast long shadows because of its lingering lament.
Those drawn close disappear when they see those that are afflicted.
Bear the burden bold some say; lay down the sword others profess.
Counsel is naught at these moments as the heart cries at the moon.
Distress and disease waltz offbeat in this thorny briar patch.
Deep groans in the spirit cannot be heard, where lies comfort?
Nonplused is God, so eternal His mercy, so sweet His balm.

Personal Reflections

_____

_____

_____

_____

_____

5

Jerusalem

One can see the lustrous desires of this burgh, forged in tumult.
This place bristles with persistent passion it fights pragmatics.
Sunlit glint upon stones, streets, walls and domes has a smell here.
The roll of humanity plays the tangled tune of living.
Times ago, it was not yet flogged by unforgiving religious structures.
Tribal people set their foot here and cried out "city of the great King."
Prophets spoke as the mouthpiece of God and tore their garments.
Poets sang songs here and packed truth in perpetual words.
But alas, the crucifixion rock and healing pools proved inadequate.
Pillars, arches, mortar and tar; cars and toots now themselves a sepulcher.
Yet for all, holiness sat here the Savior strode here and pondered here.
Walking here today, his utterances echo keenly and clearly the same.
"Love one another...believe on me...do this in remembrance of me."
Meteor showers pale in comparison to this place – oh Jerusalem.

Personal Reflections

_____

_____

_____

_____

_____

Joy

There, so I saw the event.
Elation, glee came to see.
A light tone let I out.
Yes utterances they were.
Spoke gaily, sighed lightly.
A moment was caught.
Flash indeed went the pan.
Glitz sparkled at salutation.
November dew did done.
Summer night a little light.
An occasion with smile
Funny thing this happiness
It whispers away.
Joy pounds the soul eternally.

Personal Reflections

_____

_____

_____

_____

_____

Men in Black Robes

Quieted, they approached God.
Voices stirred the soul.
Vigils and lauds banged my bones.
Chants praise and embrace the almighty.
So stand, men in black robes.
No stranger, not one in their midst.
Anyone that comes greeted as the Christ.
Pensive, passionate are moved beyond self.
Solace and solicitous are there too!
Speaking gently is their gifted balm.
Walking softly gives deference to heavenly peace.
Shallow wants as dust blown to the wind.
Celebrate the Eucharist, drink the blood.
Spirit refreshed, deed done, monks in black robes

Personal Reflections

_____

_____

_____

_____

_____

Relationships

The universe is too grand to be stuck.
This human family is too grand to be rigid.
No, not a prostitution of personal values no, not that.
Bidding is to come to the party where life's hues are painted.
Here plaids and abstracts mix, here anyone is everyone!
Keys and constraints are sharpened smooth.
Here to live without the other is painful.
Here vulgar wealth is shamed by modesty.
Here the hooks and fetters that master the flesh are set aside.
The gauging of human worth is found in the sailing of the spirit.
The dignity of the soul is preserved while the dross passes away.
Limitless is this living; pallet pleasing is its spice.
Selflessness abounds here, selfishness nailed to the cross.
So vibrates God's masterful family.

Personal Reflections

_____

_____

_____

_____

_____

Peace

Rancorous river you're not so sweet.
Stilled pools lively and deep
Waters rolled sleepy and neat
Gushed falls quieted the howl
Life lay in hammock
A drift on dosed Prozac
Meaning wonders in and out
Worry less so thoughts remain.
Even no wind in which to spit
Boiled in the cup of tin
Chaffed by blustery wind
Hide sawed so thin.
Ah, what a must.
Peace given Godly

Personal Reflections

_____

_____

_____

_____

_____

Agape

Neither, malaise or lasting happiness is this melting of self.
For such moments we ascribe to infatuation.
Eager the blood boils and the heart throbs as eyes light with desire.
Time passes and we feel pangs of sorrow, love we said, lust it was.
Intensely we look upon a friend, a sister, a brother, or strayed kin.
Moved with a sense of closeness that desire to affiliate
To break the gauntlet of misery we set a spell.
Then taste we do of some form of love well needed.
Frail we encounter our own shadow, often a bitter herb we say.
Perhaps malformed, a defective nose often uttered.
Comely, no good are loathsome comments that warped our way.
Pierced by heaven's eye our spirit is enlivened by a brave thought.
Here I am unconditionally accepted as I am.
Not fettered by form, so Christ loved, the Greeks called this agape

Personal Reflections

_____

_____

_____

_____

_____

11

Grace

This world is so little this place is so short.
Even measure that is pithy is not so strange.
Not even the uncommon has much to refrain.
This silly punch we call reality is not so striking.
Can we, thee, id or libido move consciously free?
Nope, our own burdens are our own decisions.
They are not irreconcilable for loving truth seekers.

Roots expanded can ground us in unsavory soil.
Eschew that knot by tasting unmerited favor.
That bite assuages the heart and balms the blow.
Few are resigned to this fluid and breathless flow.
Yet, it is there abundant and greener than the field.
Sensitive to this presence we bloom in God's grace.

Personal Reflections

_____

_____

_____

_____

_____

Longsuffering

Put down that untamed tiger.
Listless woe let it not linger.
Shallow grows the tepid response.
Wroth cooled in blissful repose.

Stood amidst energies afoot
Long set asunder impetuous guile
Heartstrings tug to be undone.
Eyes wonder for paths afar.

Harps enchanting call so wide.
Strides the soul for life outside
Hear remains cooled zeal unchained.
Beckons the world to honest stillness

From all that can and a little that could
Sweet is life played on strings of patience.

Personal Reflections

_____

_____

_____

_____

13

When a Nine-Year Old Sees Stars

Meteors shower the black-lit sky in
streaks that are brilliantly white.
Speed and the vastness of this display
redeem the thoughts of a nine-year old boy.

They leave big-brown eyes awe struck
and captured with pure wonderment.
"How many have you counted?"
I asked my son.

Gleefully, with quick wit and candid assurance
he softly sounded off "34."
Silence embraced the moment,
nothing else needed to be said.

This quietness milked the pure
delight of well-framed joy.

Personal Reflections

_____

_____

_____

_____

Temperance

Think about it for a moment, to be sober in thought and deed.
To hold back from over indulgence and abstain from worldly lusts
Dashing the remorse of a newly purchased luxury van is grand.
Cutting away frivolous diversion and the folly of the flagrant
Your lusts are lifted from the blackened shadow of enlargement?
Rethinking the having of all things to being moderate in all things
Think about it for a moment, the word ascetic kindled in common cant.

Surely this is a hard thing? Or is it?
Think about it for a moment people get angry when they get too fat.
They sue eateries for selling fat foods as they watch their bellies grow.
Unabashedly, they feed desire and let desire turn to vindictiveness.
Folly fills our courts as judges dismiss attempts for selfish gain.
Temperance has value His community gives place to its stay.
Restraint breaks the yoke of credit-card woe; think about it!

Personal Reflections

_____

_____

_____

_____

_____

Chairs

Chairs used to be so comfortable.
Seldom did they have bends, tilts,
bumps, lifts, levers or shaped seats.
You could plunk down in them and say ah!
Nowadays, plunking down may
be followed by ejection.
Or, at least numbered adjustments
The worst of all worlds, you could
be sold a radically contoured chair.
The pitch would be, "it is designed
especially with you in mind."
Ingratiating words considering you've
never been out of Sheboygan.
Yep, the chair was made in China.
Still some say, "Come sit awhile."

Personal Reflections

_____

_____

_____

_____

_____

16

Jazz

Basie, Benson, and Bennett.
Eckstine, Ellington, and Evans
Fragrant tunes fall from their pallet.
Can you hear the ringing in your ears?
"A Train," "Tenderly," a few of theirs
So many others, so much richness
Sweepingly, these artists paint musical
portraits with striking creative hue.
Straight ahead it can move your bones.
Fusion loosens known down beats.
Not me, ok "if you ain't got it then you
can't get it," Armstrong so said.
Raw talent, how about gifted by God?
Surely truer than that old blue note

Personal Reflections

_____

_____

_____

_____

_____

God's Brain

Slipping into imagination we find creation.
Thoughts of eternity tickle our fancy.
We deduce that God has given thought
to a structured cosmos.
It rides on reason that says knowing
is purely a cognitive affair.
Clues are sprinkled along heavens' highway.
Thus, it must be true God has a brain.

Certainly, His ways are above our ways,
so profound His brain must be!
Effectually, we think and have a brain,
God thinks and has a brain.
His brain is so much like ours.
It must be for we are created in His image.
Choked with pretense we nimbly dance
with our own images of arrogance.

Yet, what we have imagined is
captured by our own imagination.
For Jehovah has neither, body or brain.
Form, substance, and structure come
only from Him as created product.
His being is without ephemeral,
phenomenal or explainable limitations.
Passing over, residing securely in Him
are those free from dogged reasoning.

Personal Reflections

Love, Again

Love, much about it is written.
Always, stirred by the imagination
Always, lived beyond reality
Always, held as virtue untouched
Love cries aloud when torched with passion.
Tuned to sacrifice it rails against pomp
Leaping out of eternity it grabs our soul.
It turns the heart of stone to flesh.
It pours out all of itself always.
Love lives to animate life

Personal Reflections

_____

_____

_____

_____

_____

19

Pain

Pain is such an odd thing.
Sometimes it staggers emotions.
Strength is sold as an outcome.
Depth of character is forged.
Looking to conquer is now ok.
Lost is some of self.
Pain does produce paradox.
Eyes swiftly espy remorse.
Heart's elation beats gaily.
Nowhere is truth distilled.
Hindrances remain to hinder.
Proof of the fray does stay.
One did make heaven open.
Yeshua still arises with good.

Personal Reflections

_____

_____

_____

_____

_____

Glory

We hear it in titles.
We read it in books.
Songs often sing of it.
It strikes us as elation.
Filled the heavens it has.
It comes forth with resolve.
Often it brings needed change.
It can animate life profoundly.
Holler it out we should.
Even reserved folks need try.
With vehemence let it "rain."
Whim and fancy find place.
Others and I observe it.
God's glory it's everywhere.

Personal Reflections

_____

_____

_____

_____

_____

21

Green

Green is such a beautiful color.
Multitudes of shades grace it presence.
It is seen everywhere with little appreciation.
Yet, it assails us in numerous mixtures.
In black there is often green, likewise in blue.
Seen in potted plants and men's pants
Oh, and don't forget beautiful, abounding trees.
Flow it does even through women's sleeves.
Never though seen in sweet eating ants

Personal Reflections

_____

_____

_____

_____

_____

Hurt

Hurt just sneaks up on you.
It catches you off guard.
Sometimes it pounds you like anguish.
Other times it pierces like a sword.
It dulls your sense of being.
And, weighs those weary steps
On the other hand..
Yes, there's always an, on the other hand.
Especially, if you're an Episcopalian
Hurt is short lived.
Hang around for days, it usually doesn't.
Heart soon reasons in another direction.
Hurt so lifts the eyes.
Let the new flight prevail, let it!

Personal Reflections

_____

_____

_____

_____

_____

Hope

Let not any man steal it away.
Guard it closely hold it deep in your bosom.
Decide that it is ever present in your life.
When roll in tides of bleakness.
Notice how it lifts your spirit.

No, this is not the wings' of money.
It is not the rampantly indulged self.
Rather it is that moment, that perpetual second.
When out of the glare of despair there springs hope.

Now, what can lie undone?
May I dare say nothing?
Hope in God, there all things are possible.

Personal Reflections

_____

_____

_____

_____

_____

Elders

Elders are such a curious lot.
No, not the type that is up in age.
Rather, these are the folks that serve in churches.
Most think they are divinely appointed; usually,
some time before the foundation of the world.
Carrying with them such regal rank they love to
put holiness into those that are less holy.
Commonly, that is everyone!
Such function is done with pure sterility.
Neither joy, nor laughter, nor winsome smile
cross the wizened crevices of their leathery tile.
Graciously, pass over visible limitations
Most of what they do is served by selfless love.
Granted so says "Everyman," it is somewhat!

Personal Reflections

_____

_____

_____

_____

_____

Denial

Getting all of our wants fulfilled, that is our nature.
Struggling in this endeavor to the point of distress
That is our nature.
Our own bigness must be satiated.
Often we cast aside contentment.
The aim is purely to gain.
Vulgar are the expenses that follow.
Ruined may be the dignity of freedom.
Now, financial shackles rule life.
Peaceable escape is found in a different view.
It sets aside the press of burning consumption.
Words of this path have been heard for ages.
Denial of self, death to self, deny thy self.
Thus the soul is renewed, life is potent.

Personal Reflections

_____

_____

_____

_____

_____

Healing

Healing comes forth in many shapes and sizes.
You can buy it from your local doctor or in a bottle.
Finding it in exercise is possible bending joints is viable.
Changing the diet can sometimes do wonders sometimes.
How about mind over matter? What if I'm losing my mind?
Occasionally, an elder will pray for you if the "links" permit.
Retreating to a high and dry climate helped my uncle.
Others charge ahead believing in advanced technology.
Therapy may help if the condition is psychosomatic.
Do what you can with what you have - pull yourself up!
Even use bootstraps if necessary – that's the last word.
Or is it? From the lips do fall prayerful concerns
Now, God is in the works, healing touches your body.
If it touches your soul, greater is the miracle therein.

Personal Reflections

_____

_____

_____

_____

_____

Heroes

Heroes don't stand in the limelight or sit in the dull-shaded woods of oblivion.
They don't out of compulsion reach for stars or grab at the gauntlet of jaded success.
Often they are found where the meek hang their hats, where mercy bends a knee.
They don't disdain disagreement or balk at the jargon that promotes exchange.
Rather these people engage convictions and lift high the mantle of sacrifice.

Personal Reflections

_____

_____

_____

_____

_____

Waiting

Waiting can be frustrating.
It holds within all that wants out of you.
Provoke it and it proves agitating.
Neighbors may appear bothersome.
Friends may look like foes.
That guy next to you is sleeping.
Nope, you can't go anywhere.
You're stuck on the bullet train to Paris.
Stopped dead in your tracks by workers
Union members are blocking the rails.
French officials ponder then drink some wine.
We did move a few feet, slowly.
A lady laughed with words "first time?"
A merry heart rejoices the spirit even when waiting.

Personal Reflections

_____

_____

_____

_____

_____

Touch

Orgasmic are the depths of the creator's touch.
Completely undone, that was how I was left.
Easily, it has found my most furtive thought.
Not brashly did the universe unfold before me.
Now, I touch the moon from my bedroom.

Personal Reflections

_____

_____

_____

_____

_____

War

No advocate of death or destruction.
Neither the naiveté of glory
So lay words on this pallet.
Deafen the jingles of jingoism.
Political platitudes here earn no merit.
Preservation of the "way of life," pops up.
The good become corrupted.
The corrupted become politicians.
Leaders, lust to carve up the world.
Into, "haves and haves not"
That's where you and I live.
Mangled, are many of us.
Bruised with anguish, are others.
Come on let's beat a few ships into plowshares.

Personal Reflections

_____

_____

_____

_____

_____

Working

There is honor in all work.
To work with one's brain is cool.
To work with one's hands is cool.
Often, it is hard to find a place to work.
More often, and rightly so, work finds us.
Some work to find big money.
Not doing this bodes for an angry spouse.
Doing it often wounds one's life.
Yet, we persevere, to make something.
To produce something, it is a natural bent.
Then lift the process.
In the doing let there be great joy.
Heartily, vigorously move to the outcome.
The reward, Immanuel driven, so it should be.

Personal Reflections

_____

_____

_____

_____

_____

Aside

Don't find me captured by un-assailed virtue.
Looking on thrones where rings seal fates.
Not there either, not on tiers of frail success.
Look askance at the garland of roses.

Pondering, reflecting, and chewing on other moments.
Don't silly yourself with the pomp of priggish heroes.
Step aside the veil of headline or overdone adulation.
When the wind blows the hardest,
those with peace of soul stand the longest.
There are beliefs and actions of an eternal sort.

Personal Reflections

_____

_____

_____

_____

_____

Capture

Rembrandt did this better than all others who put oil on canvass.
Looking into the eyes of his subject he captured his very essence.
Those things that made for life were then bathed in color and form.
Never did one ask, what is this? Or, where is the top?
Rather they stood in awe and remarked this is the "Prodigal Son."
Sandburg, read the magnificent stories of human existence.
He marked pages with little slips of paper.
He must have been sipping the ravishing content of the moment?
Now, he could do what he did better than most, dirty paper.
Today, a host of folks strive to capture carbs and fats.
Obese our bodies become but "our souls remain lean."
Try a different tilt, lightly taste of bliss eternal.
Rapture will fill your being.
Capturing Godly pleasure such is life's aim.

Personal Reflections

_____

_____

_____

_____

_____

Combat

Combat levels everything.
Neophytes mature boldly.
Brazen bastards from the
south Bronx turn to milk toast.
That trepid boy from Wichita
saves your life at his expense.
Tortured tissue flays the sky.
Bones dried litter the byway.
Strongholds though are destroyed.
Ugly rouges are deposed.
Lights of another kind can shine?
Faintly then, let it stir only on the
dim glimmer of shadowy trenches.
For combat levels everything.

Personal Reflections

_____

_____

_____

_____

_____

35

Contemplation

Contemplation is such a rich experience.
A panorama of events is at your disposal.
You can climb Everest or swim the Channel.
You can resolve the irresolvable.
Dwelling in the bosom of God is divine.

Personal Reflections

_____

_____

_____

_____

_____

Daddy, No Rhyme

Dad, your poem just doesn't rhyme.
It has no meter, there isn't any pattern.
There's no sound that makes it shine.
So sad, no rime, no time and no chime
Not undone by savvy son's pithy chide.
I entered the fray to make a poem with rhyme.
Task at hand, I grabbed hold of this rocky climb.
Line upon line no words with concord do I hide.
With tonal form they now lie upon these lines.
Good the self-denial to taste a pedantic trail.
Good the sacrifice to serve the joy of another.
Remarks arise, this is wordsmith gone awry.
Judge not, from him who suffered unjust rile
Son delight with words alike; if nay make hay

Personal Reflections

_____

_____

_____

_____

_____

Death Comes Suddenly

Death comes ever so suddenly
Yet, it is not without surprise.
We all feel its inexorable force.
Darkened moods lick the soul.
Joys abandon oh so tempting.
In youth it passed in shadows.
Grey year's find it everywhere.
It falls from the lips of friends.
It paces the homes of loved ones.
It haunts us in living memories.
A calm tune of remorse is played.
Lingers the grief of he who is gone
Now, what is left some do say.
Life truly alive the Savior replies.

Personal Reflections

_____

_____

_____

_____

_____

38

Down

Something did matter that I cannot see.
It was driven in me valued by eternity.
Looking down the road to new byways
Future calls beyond the grievous mist.
Senses were tuned to the pricks of risk.
Watch for eyes a bright there I did stay.
Stone the languid past from refrain abstain.
Now hold a salted and piercing interlude.
Spiced by bitter herbs this place passes.
A sorrowful sting sets emotions a stir.
That look those casting eyes were mine.
No need to grovel in a moody pall.
I caught that loathsome down.
Turned I heavenward all groans.

Personal Reflections

_____

_____

_____

_____

_____

Eagles Never Cry

Beyond the edge of elation eagles never cry.
Over plaguing taunts eagles' tear every dry.
The sweep of storm never stays its sail.
Now a time when many look dimly up trail
There glides this bird with eyes towards water.
Drafts up, down and around it stood still.
Not a blink at remorse or wink at loss.
Aplomb in all, it was undisturbed in its airy dominion,
Rock one for this grandeur, for this tranquil flight.
Straighten bent knees and lock onto an emotional soar.
Hold nothing, dim nothing, and let worry slip to the pit.
Living without weary is so savored by every pore.
Mounted up that's the key on those wings of the eagle.
Here I live, there I be, how fix ye this conundrum?

Personal Reflections

_____

_____

_____

_____

_____

Fantastic

Swept away with something marvelous
There goes the breath that brought life.
Moments pass and there you stand.
Those feet of yours, are they moving?
Perhaps, you are frozen in awe?
Then it begins to sink in.
You are observing something out of antiquity.
Pondering it, it almost takes on life.
Simmering in your brain meaning unfolds.
Passion is excited and remorse knows no place.
The feeling is to leap from one's shoes.
Yet, the gaze remains fixed, steady and absorbed.
Belief wanders across the sands of years, what can it be?
From the crown of the Savior it is a thorn!

Personal Reflections

_____

_____

_____

_____

_____

Fathers

Fathers often get a bad rap.
Often, it is ill conceived.
Filled with the neurosis of others
Don't shift an eye in that direction.
For who knows the heart of man?
Certainly, not the casual observer,
never the distant pedantic.

Rather fathers know themselves.
Some well, some not so well.
Differences though tend to blur over time.
Their energies, their actions loom tall.
Not perfect just tall.
It's as if they're scraping the
mist off of nauseating absurdities.

Many find the race is run differently.
The weave of life is not often blistered
by bright-august hues.
Threads sown gaily seldom highway
their personal, well chiseled passage.
Humility can dance around the
repulse of vaunted vainglories.

I know not this to be true of all fathers.
For some, the best thing they do is die.

Personal Reflections

Fields

Some have called these places Flanders, the
Argonne, Belleau Woods, or Heartbreak Ridge
In our own country do you remember Gettysburg?
In many instances men ran at each other.
Or, perhaps, one group charged another.
In any case, shouts of triumph may have been heard.
Mixed they were with shrieks of pain, haunting groans
And breaths breathed upon lips of blood.
In all of these places rest the placid shadows of agony.
Mostly though mothers wept and wept again.
Fathers hold a deep, hollow tone – my son, my son.
Need I go farther? Surely, you've figured it out?
Doff the cap with reverence. Hang the
head when on this dirt we call battlefields.

Personal Reflections

_____

_____

_____

_____

_____

Goodness

Requirements for goodness are not to be found.
No certification, no schooling, no none are necessary.
Some teach me the way show me the path.
Neither requisites need to be undertaken.
Embracing this marvelous Spiritual fruit is fitting.
Goodness relishes the state of being good.
It demands no special polish or inflated prose.
It calls forth mercy and kindness.
The doing inevitably follows the being.
This isn't hard to grasp, then why make it so.
Intellectual constraint holds no high call here.
Contrary, contrary it may be to the fallow self.
Lift back the furrowed brow tilt back the neck.
Do you see it? Divine goodness is thine!

Personal Reflections

_____

_____

_____

_____

_____

Wind

Teamed with Spirit, I arose and saw the wind.
Blew by me, it whispered and sung through the hollow
Messages were cool, dampened by mist, whetted by time
So close I stood to roar and tumult, peace and comfort
Not raged upon, or set adrift by thirsty howl.
Surpassing the womb and wont of nature's guile
By the moment, some essence is spared, quite enough.
Lower no sail, batten no hatches, leave no quarter.
There remain, countenance this swirl.
Now and again ride the wind and stand to the snap.
Fury or breeze neither holds to refrain thyself.
They arch their way through the marrow of existence.
Why not some of us?
Why not spin uniquely frames of life?

Personal Reflections

_____

_____

_____

_____

_____

Inconsistencies

Inconsistencies abound in life.
Spring is neither, hot or cold.
Does that mean it is luke warm?
Some days though are hot.
Others are genuinely chilly.
Some live where snow prevails.
Occasionally, folks will say
"we had no Spring."
Give the existentialist some sway.
They spring into the moment.
Post-modernist decry limits.
Spring is an abysmal illusion.
Generally, though it does persist.
Let this then remain – rain!

Personal Reflections

_____

_____

_____

_____

_____

Inconvenience

People don't like to be inconvenienced.
They want to be left to their own devices.
They enjoy the thrill of individual effort.
Their own outcome fully materialized.
That is a grand moment, a pure delight.
Yet, in all of this there remains a catch.
You sidestepped an important request.
A tug in another direction is discarded.
That intuitive hunch is left undone.
Reasons were not loosely woven.
Haunting though the conscience
rings on the door bell of your mind.
Dip a shoulder you lighten the load.
Certainly, this is now and ever more.

Personal Reflections

_____

_____

_____

_____

_____

Heavenliness

How circumspect is your world view?
Does it embrace unfeigned zeal?
Can you see yourself beyond limits?
Or are you roped to the digits of your p.c.?
If so, spend a moment in heavenliness.
There unbridled knowing warmly unfolds.
One could debase with it reasoning.
Or, ponder it as inexplicable beauty.
Sprinkle the arena with some senses.
If I could only see or feel it you say.
Typical, for such is our primal nature.
No, you're not there with such works.
Rather, you're moved.
Into all that ever was or ever could be.

Personal Reflections

_____

_____

_____

_____

_____

Marine

Sing that song from the "Halls of Montezuma."
Raise that melody from the "shores of Tripoli."
Sure bravado rings and a little salt stings.
It's the boot up, well you know where for a little zing.

Hold bravely to that gun, oops that's the one for fun.
Love that rifle, walk so tall and a casual piss at the sun.
No heroes at the bar, they isolate and stand afar.
Moods run thick, a giddy quip or deep as blackened tar.

Now history runs long with this Corps.
Longer than any others that knocked at battle's door.
Dustier than books where blood has dripped
Iwo Jima or Kha Shan, lots of lips still zipped.

Politicians, you know are quick to fry the flesh.
Marines' expendable easily dashed to any test.
Every helmet strapped on, every head commits.
Die for others or brass in the ass, whom of you does this?

Personal Reflections

_____

_____

_____

_____

Spring

Spring the vibrancy of life.
Is this what you want?
Spring nature's renewed energy?
Is this what you want?
Perhaps it is better to dust off the soul?
For there reigns peace and joy.

Personal Reflections

_____

_____

_____

_____

Glances

Glances, I now understand are potent.
They can pierce any veil of protection.
Correctly, perceived truth can prevail.
Incorrectly, known pain in pervaisive.
Considered I results of my own eyes.
"When you look at me, it grades against me"
"I don't like it, I don't ever want to come
to your house again." Heard I such words.
Son, it was who spoke so sharply.
Crestfallen, I breathed lightly from the wound.
Lingered, woes from that moment
Dejection is lost in the art of the creator.
Supplications reaped; "Dad, I'm sorry for what I said."
Forgiveness was his, reconciliation ours.

Personal Reflections

_____

_____

_____

_____

_____

Markets

Stocks, bonds, and commodities
they are all financial markets.
The common cant goes something like this:
buy now, buy more and believe in America.
Fiscal folks, have to say that.
It is for your good, they say.
Ultimately, it only lines their wallets.
Your good is sweetly sacrificed when
markets explode into a scarlet abyss.
Citizen, look askance at pocket pickers.

Personal Reflections

_____

_____

_____

_____

_____

Numbness

Numbness looked me smack in the eye.
It did not tickle a single fancy or elicit a single emotion.
It simply seemed to exist in vacuous space.
Yet, it was chiseled there in the midst of human exchange.
How could this happen?
How could the animate become inanimate?
Abandoning ultimate intentions for a faceless stare
Leaving behind vision, meaning, and family, friends and living life
A once lively soul becomes stained and dulled by inane commerce.
Culpable, some would say, are the drones playing the money game.
Yet, here does one place oneself on the spicy block of sweet success.
Faintly, a hand is extended, the till is rung, and profits are sung.
Someone smiles with such marketed, timely and lucrative stuff.
Stilled personage still sits in timeless limbo waiting for the bliss.

Personal Reflections

_____

_____

_____

_____

_____

Overcoming

Overcoming the limits of pain there is the wonder of joy.
Living is not amassed by the feeble question of "how much?"
Feeble minds will only lay hold of a fat wallet or round belly.
"Increasing," is often thought of as the way to bountifulness.
Cannot be disguised though is that desire to get to the other side.
What it may be, we know not, we just seek to be there.
Set in motion is natural energy to overcome challenges.
Now, our eyes gaze at the present and look to the future.
Target a prize – could it be renewed health or fresh kinship?
Elevation of spirit is perhaps greater than the fruit of overcoming.
Recklessly, we can explode with joy and jubilation.
Lay constraints the jealous, envious or dunderheaded will say.
Why even begin to hinder something effusive and uncertain?
The wind of the Spirit blows through your life – ever let it be!

Personal Reflections

_____

_____

_____

_____

_____

Phenomenal

Out of the shackles of thought springs uniqueness.
Often, we don't even recognize it!
Gestalt, is it about that sudden burst of light?
Nope, often such sudden flash dims beyond recognition.
Does paradoxing the ridiculous bring breath-taking truth?
Nope, bash the absurd, that bottomless pit leads nowhere.
Twist in your chair for a moment.
Let the clash of an inexplicable event ring in your soul.
Does it seem uncomfortable and sweat provoking?
If so, capture something you have not previously known.
If not, you're dead, good; there remain at least for a while.

Personal Reflections

_____

_____

_____

_____

_____

Riches

"Gold and silver are cankered."
Yet, there remain so many so trusting.
Putting the life of the soul in deception
Oppressing many from their own oppression
Living as powerful; yet, so soon withered.
Drawn from the tales of time was fame.
High the name low the bowels of mercy.
Dim lights overshadow glowing adulation.
Hold back more then, lean is life.
Shaken by the toil of limitless hectoring
Now other names become salient.
Self-promotion is easily bitten by frailty.
Step hindered, breath slowed, vile the virus.
The eternal One now lovingly beckons again.

Personal Reflections

_____

_____

_____

_____

_____

Sacrifice

Seldom do you hear the word used.
Less yet, do you see it in action.
Nowadays, there is much ado about self.
Rich folks like to write about their rich dads.
Most of them never had a rich dad.
They had one that taught them about
love, compassion, care and sacrifice.
They traded that dad for one that taught
exploitation, avarice, and disdain for e.e. cummings.
Oops, I let the word out, did you notice?
Sacrifice that is we lay down the "self."
Effectually we're crucified to that old nature.
The benefit is for others – exclaim, let us!
"We are our brother's keeper."

Personal Reflections

_____

_____

_____

_____

_____

Searching

What is it that has one's heart.
Can it be the wealth of nations?
No, this leaves people shallow, in want of more.
Can it be the pride of fame?
No, this is fleeting, bereft of true glory.
Can it be the sum of all knowledge?
No, for facts change, they limit what can be known.
Can it be chasing the hominid?
No, for one fragment quickly supersedes the past.
The past is vacuous; thus, will soon be this minute.
Then it must be love that chains one heart to another.
Nothing lasting there only lust that quickly fades with wrinkles.
Vanity it is to search for something that captures our essence.
A renewed heart that is shaped by God; there eternity is held.

Personal Reflections

_____

_____

_____

_____

_____

Small

Small is good.
It means better living.
The house is smaller.
Accommodations are unique.
Toilets, sinks and floors
are of far better quality.
If on wheels, no taxes
I know stuff still prevails
Garbage cans are a quick fix.
No bedroom for visitors.
A tent and cot works.
Complainers, send them
to the local red-light motel.
Now, there's real luxury.
Small is good.

Personal Reflections

_____

_____

_____

_____

_____

Art is Home

Piccolo is his favorite instrument, played mostly in B flat.
Knock on the door, coffee is on – Amaretto, Art is home.
No blue note from him, sounds are cool and refreshing.
Conversation is informed, spontaneous, dignified and encouraging.
Come on in, set a while, drop those shoulders, relax Art is home.

Pizza nay, let's do Chinese, flickering candles, and plumb wine.

Only moments, only years, heart's sweetness forges relationship.
Free as a breeze, but yoked with you beyond ephemeral times.
Darkened, low, and unwound by joy that's fine.
Not the slippery sort, not sordid in tales, but rich in expression.
Therapists are pierced with fear by such character, by such life.
Shrinks find their jobs restructured, clerking becomes their resolve.
Quietude is his friend, solace is found with others, relax Art is home.

Personal Reflections

_____

_____

_____

_____

_____

Directions

Directions often hinder us.
We turn left, right or go straight ahead.
Sometimes we even head from
whence we have just come.
Confusing our personal schemes may be?
Striving for the main stay, leaves
are still filtered from the heavens.
Clarify that direction so is the call.
Vision, mission, strategy; those will do.
Set the goal, achieve the objective
so is measured personal progress.
Embroiled in this mish mash,
step into the comfort of spiritual rest.
Notice, there you're different.

Personal Reflections

_____

_____

_____

_____

_____

Fire

Slim are chances that many would live from fire.
No embers glow where work is labor.
No zeal is manifest where life's tide is damned.
Shortened are the crescendos that move all that is.
Halted, truncated are acts that turn the downside up.
Images and thoughts may hold you there – numb.
Lifting that cigar butt, dam that's heavy
But, the spark remains, it haunts you, it is you.
It penetrates all your doing, even veiled in disguise.
It is there perpetually created as part of your being.
Embracing this flame, living becomes recreated.
Risks are there, softened by massaging grace.
Caught now is the guest, here it be, laid before you.
Hold to that zest and burn brightly like the bush.

Personal Reflections

_____

_____

_____

_____

_____

Loss of a Parent

The phone call came early – touching another's ear.
The message came simply and came direct.
Tones of sorrow spoke an abundance of meaning.
"Your mother lies dying in the hospital."

Riding to the airport brought the tears of loss.
One more hug, one more kiss, was all that was wished.
Embraces lost forever enforces the value of mother.
Remorse is assuaged by transcendent tranquility.

Hospital halls were aseptic, waxed hard were the tiles.
Clutter sat still at every corner, quiet loomed loud.
Buzzed into where I had to go, sat still the room.
Curtains drawn, darkness in the air – ouch the gloom

She laid still, body warm, eyes shut, heart beating by machine.
Data ticked off the monitor, bright and color-coded.
Bandages, bottles, tubes and medications worked for naught.
All that was mom was truly gone.

Grief cut deeply, to the core of my being.
It lingered in waves, ebbing and flowing.
I wanted it to be enough, shallow that desire.
Laments softened knowing paradise is her retreat.

Gravesite prepared flowers and friends.
Pastor's words compassionate, embracing and true.
Dirt tossed on the coffin lowering into the ground.
Wrenching sorrow; ultimately, we'll touch her with pure delight.

Miracles

For some strange reason, miracles do happen.
Supernatural events piercing the natural order
A sea did not have to be split, but it was.
Walking on water did not have to occur but it did.
Time doesn't have to stop but it has.
Humanity has observed such things.
All such is poetic illusion, some have said.
Yet, their next breath may be inexplicable.
Skeptical, many hold back, tacit are their lips.
Uproariously thankful they should have been.
After all, blind have received and dead raised.
Intricate, spontaneous miracles still happen.
One, then another, and another are touched.
Circumstances changed and most unexpectedly.
Thank God!

Personal Reflections

_____

_____

_____

_____

_____

Studs

Foot upon ground, never I walked upon before.
Not upon grass, concrete, plastic or mud but upon studs.
Studs soaked with the sweet incense of machine oil.
Surely, a hundred years has passed above them.
None looked down, but all found their solid ground.
Upholding machines, tools, teachers, and things made.
Tricks of the trade were learned upon these studs.
Hands of learning manipulated the weaving of steel above them.
Windows have gone, flown is the merit of achievement.
Technical showcases stand now removed.
These studs are simply waves of wood echoing past performance.
Quiet, my father walked here, ah!, now so do I.

Personal Reflections

_____

_____

_____

_____

_____

Abbey

There are certain places where everyone should try to stand quietly.
You don't need to expound great truths.
Rather the facts at hand dictate that you don't need to do anything.
You never need to utter the word efficiency.
Contending with friend on issues of the day – leave it way behind.
Maudlin sentimentalism dropped at the door.
Have you made it inside yet?
That is, have you opened the portals and walked inside an Abbey?
Have you wound around hallways and found a Holy place?
There are many of them, intriguing rooms to isolated-tiny nooks.
Lastly, slip into the chapel.
Caution can be cast aside here you can commune – earnestly.
Free of guile you sense an ultimate encounter.
In an elevated-lost moment the breath of God blew through you.

Personal Reflections

_____

_____

_____

_____

_____

Deep

Deep in the hallow of being, there resides something.
It is beyond the effable, here the earth is filled.
Here there is nothing artificial, nothing sterile.
Here there are no moods, treasures or fabrications.
Here there are things eternal, compelling to the soul.
Here life is nipped at, tension eased and good fattened.
Here that which is known is paled by uncertainty.
Coming to the star is glows in the light,
wishes are no longer afar.
Coming to a moment is arriving at eternity.
Sounds that penetrate, words that pierce were here.
Moody dialogue and vibrant harps played the stay.
Ave Maria is sung here.
So sets the tunes for life, deep.

Personal Reflections

_____

_____

_____

_____

_____

67

Fidelity

Fear and anger you deceptively bare.
Portentous moments foment despair.
Times twist your encumbered cares.
Doubt and thought need repair.
Fidelity finds Yahweh there!

Personal Reflections

_____

_____

_____

_____

_____

Silence

Stripped of all that can be borne
Naked within, no pomp or pretense without
Flowing in silence remains a refined fate.
Gone are the abrasive, the gong and the bong.
Hidden away are solipsism, unrest and that
nagging need to know what is best.

Kindred spirits, brightened minds, soulful
Hearts embrace this exclusive time.

Where else could one be?
Where else would one go?
Different voyages may stoke lamentable moans.
Movement creases the fold of silence.
Out of this non-noised state comes a true cast.
A taste of the triune wedding has been found.

Personal Reflections

_____

_____

_____

_____

_____

Mercy

Have you received something that you did not deserve?
Cry mercy.
Did goodness intervene in a way that lifted your life?
Cry mercy.
Did kindness knock on your door unannounced?
To you, a hand extended that brought comfort.
In these cry mercy.
Now comes your chance to lift another's plight.
Your wisely tuned years inspire the down trodden.
A just act relieves suffering.
A loving disposition builds brotherhood.
Freely, you yoke yourself to another man's burden.
Perversely, you suddenly shout, what's in it for me?
"Blessed are the merciful, for they shall receive mercy."

Personal Reflections

_____

_____

_____

_____

_____

Seventy

Seventy is such a fine number, I like it!
I heard a gentleman talk about it.
His utterances were, "married seventy years,
the Bataan death march," and related thoughts.
A woman spoke gleefully about her seventy years on earth.
Her doctor remarked, "how good she looked at seventy."
People who are seventy talk about how good they feel,
a recent adventure, a new found love or eating sushi.
It's exhilarating.
People who are sixty talk about their lost tennis game,
their third divorce, constipation or eating oat meal.
It's depressing.
Seventy carries with it a quick step into the future.
Sixty carries a lament, why bother with that number?

Personal Reflections

_____

_____

_____

_____

_____

71

Person

A.M. rings in with pleasantry.
True words reflect true being.
Upbeat thoughts contain joy and presence.
Dropped are elements void of fragrance.
Pictured are eyes straight with honesty.
No desire to sow discord no none seen.
Moving beyond any single past
There strikes this time to try life.
Some reservation may remain.
Beyond that is newly tingled life.
Bringing forth prodded expression
Where there is truth there is freedom.
Keys are found in the onward press.
Emotions click forward, arising inspired.

Personal Reflections

_____

_____

_____

_____

_____

Kick the Tomb

Stone rolled away, years vacant the hole.
Dark, musty is the cavern of stories.
Angels once addressed forth comers.
Shroud once adorned his body.
Lay there, he did, bereft of breath.
The mosaic of his legacy shades
this contemporary human family.
Stuck are crafty-sheep clothed wolves.
Long is the immutable tomb.
Pitched perfect were roads and gardens.
Quieted were doubts and bantering.
Age ending he will be there.
Day beginning he is here.
Kick the tomb, break the wall.
The Jesus God has risen!

Personal Reflections

_____

_____

_____

_____

Listening

Bygone moments of silence stir the soul.
Now there is the essence of inner space.
Rocked by something real, I saw a voice.
Forever, that tone is there; yet I am not.
Evanescent; though, perfect in duration.

Personal Reflections

_____

_____

_____

_____

_____

Dispassionate

Human experiences are salted with passion.
What else so flavors the friction of exchange?
Many though find no such pleasure here.
Even those closest to the clan are disabused.
Cool dispassion smites them and their actions.
No reason, no note, no word for their errors.
It' so easy, without faces, and without what if

Reasonable stanchions they fall upon.
Such is their cool, desensitized conscience.
Cleanly they will claim victory in lesser rings.
Confessors of no extreme here are placed.
It's not willow weep for me, it's for them,
Those who are duly centered

By long chance and by short meadows
they gain their tribe.
Straight of face, dour, without blink,
there they lay their frame.

This soul has fallen upon spikes.
It is goodly fat for the experience.

Personal Reflections

_____

_____

_____

Away

Don't be so quick to set aside sweetened bliss.
Acrid speech freely drips from sterile lips.
Seldom thou, does it please the palate.
Don't be so prone to lend life to facile living.
Watch your moorings; don't let them be whitened.
Don't be so quick to gratify the slow belly.
Such fling flattens the spry step.
Watch your own peace, mind your own prejudice.
Few keenly discern past or new sails set.
Why limit then vague or shaped realities?
Why pursue only times shed fast?
Why remain steeped in tide less tempting?
Now in the midst of unveiled toil and revealed joy
Hold back scented scorn, bust yokes and relish life.

Personal Reflections

_____

_____

_____

_____

_____

Shack

A shack stands tall on the island of Mindanao.
Nothing noteworthy in construction
Rather plain overall with tin roof and thin walls.
One doubts any Westerner would enter therein?
Never open by day, at night it bulges with friends.
Elbow to elbow stand joy-filled participants.

Heated, thick and fragrant is the melodic air.
Sweat boils from face to floor.
None though ever ponder the door.
Fellowship strokes the bonds of brotherhood.
Truly not a shack at all rather a church you see.
It stands tall in the jungles of Mindanao.

Personal Reflections

_____

_____

_____

_____

_____

Solitude

At the core of being is the beauty of solitude.
Multitudes shun this embrace.
Theirs is the constancy of purely natural relationships.
This space is not for eternity, it is for reflective-pristine moments.
Revel for this time, it shouldn't escape you, if you dare the breach.
Fighting it through power or pleasure leaves you undone
The drums beat on, echoes still call where do you want to play?
Standing on the edge of this blacktop
is not enough for this greater game.
Cold and hollow will remain inside if no engagement is made.
The step beyond this cord is the road now widened.
Stretched and drawn out in the quiet amidst the crowd.
Unaggravated, without fear, now the Transcendent is touched.
Superior to anything and all, now you live – aglow.

Personal Reflections

_____

_____

_____

_____

_____

Three

Three, it is such a marvelous moment.
Some would say it's a year.
Nay, only a moment
A gleeful time excited by the bounce in a step.
Enchanted by the words that say daddy or mommy
Winsome, exuberant and laughter that bubbles with life
End around these times some would proffer.
Smiles crack though and faded eyes sparkle.
As the mind sweeps to the past when a son says,
Daddy love you, or a daughter says mommy want you.
There was something that lasted forever.
There was something that passed in a flash.
There was something that flavored life.
Three, catch it!

Personal Reflections

_____

_____

_____

_____

_____

Death

Death is a gut-wrenching, heart rendering event.
It comes blistering into life with tormented screams.
Then, finality
It lingers with waves of hope and depths of despair.
Then, finality
Silently, unannounced – there's no warning.
Then, finality
Neither youth or perfect health hinder its touch.
Some try to avoid its arrival, "it can't happen to me."
Others, lift their head asserting, "take me I'm ready."
Controlling that last exhale is found futile.
Controlling much of anything is rather futile.
Why not throw yourself into a grand plan?
Death does have its season and so do you.

Personal Reflections

_____

_____

_____

_____

_____

Rumble on Padre

Between canyon walls that you adore
Behind the lapping waves that tranquilize some
There the knee drops, hallowed utterances reach heaven.
Mass or morass, peace rides at the core of his being.
Unchecked his unbridled joy, his love unconditional
You've met him search the moment look to the breach.
Served, washed feet and painted the steed has he.
Fed the hungry and well weaved the frayed fabric.
Danced to the notes of lively or less a composer
Little has escaped him; eyes remain without jade.
Decide he does without trepidation.
Easy confidence, a spry humility rolls with him.
Work anew begins another day – off that way.
Rumble on Padre, rumble on

Personal Reflections

_____

_____

_____

_____

_____

Caprock

On the Caprock there is beauty.
Some might say it's flat and ugly.
Others pop off it is windy and dry.
Remaining on this blustery brown
rock – there is beauty.
No, you don't have the great peaks.
Roaring rivers are not necessary.
Oceans spanning the globe are
gorgeous - such is not the Caprock.
Here are browns, beiges; some greens
Reddish brown dust can pall the sky.
It is all okay – maybe perfect!
I know this for the God creator
has laid his hand to this land.

Personal Reflections

_____

_____

_____

_____

_____

Plumbing

Who plumbs the depths of the mind?
We passage the caverns of discovery.
Without hindrance, we seek resolve.
To finger the fullness of whom we are.
Answers aglow well within pure sight
We exalt the nature of unfolded being.
Then something peculiar happens.
We see the darkened brow of humanity.
We've peeked at expanded indulgence.
Fears begin to grip the thought stream.
"I don't like who I am, that sly nature."
Guile and deception finger us!
The God above all kings stills before us.
All that is, is his; wholeness there reigns.

Personal Reflections

_____

_____

_____

_____

_____

Mockery

People will behold a painting of the ages.
They'll laugh and say "it's black and dark."
A radiant diamond is laid in their palm.
A little snicker rolls from their lips.
It must be fake, look there's a flaw.
Why lay straw before a fine gem?
A Nobel novelist gifts a signed book.
It's not an adventure tale, she scoffs.
Responding in this way is baffling.
It serves no purpose, neither gain.
A child visits heaven and returns.
His pure comments twist our mind.
Aloof laughter says it's an illusion.
Praise the unknown it sets faith afire.

Personal Reflections

_____

_____

_____

_____

_____

Eyes

Eyes to behold are beautiful.
They can take away your breath.
The colors are magnificent.
Eyes sparkle and light up life.
Hope and elation leaps from them.
From afar they connect with you.
You're spirited into a new kinship.
Looking into them finds the soul.
Forthwith shines purity.
Momentarily, it halts you.
A slight gaze views new images.
They dance across your mind like,
the ballerina glides over the stage.
Eyes preserve us.

Personal Reflections

_____

_____

_____

_____

_____

Vision

Blurred by aimless toil
Tainted by distress
Bent by broken promises
Derided by scorners
Scorned by mockers
Dismissed by pragmatists
Lampooned by prattlers
Poked to depart
Pressed to abandon
Push back, pump iron
Renew energy
Lift high ideas
They will fly
Vision maps tomorrow.

Personal Reflections

_____

_____

_____

_____

_____

The Church Rep

She came to my house bearing bread.
The Christ-Mass was in the air.
Shared her story, told of her church
Her life was rich, her fate timely.
Interesting these throws of providence.
Pacts of peace they promote.
Not dangled the sweep of void argot
Not dangled words of style or form
No distance, no façade, this rep had it.
Hope balanced with tomorrow's eternity.
The sense this made was real.
Bygone is the mist of frail quietness.
Let the good brought by this rep raid life.
Standards seen, set in perfect freedom.

Personal Reflections

_____

_____

_____

_____

_____

Art

Art is the breath of God,
breathed into society,
to provide it with beauty.

Personal Reflections

_____

_____

_____

_____

_____

Recognition

Living sounds come forth.
Dancing on the notions of life
Played upon the flute of your soul
Tunes change your consciousness
Not with roar.
Quietly they pierce finely hewed organs.
Recognize this?
It is the fragrance of Yahweh

Personal Reflections

_____

_____

_____

_____

_____

No

I, nor all that is love would stand in your way.
Who are you that command the much, the little?
Not an ember warming life or words fitly spoken.
Not an effusive reflection not a drone in the night.
You're the steady epitaph the ever-running story.
You're the one without peer, without reproach.
To all, to any, to one you are the "no, not I."

Of course, this must be you've chosen it.
Assured is this tack, this rightful course.
Sails set un-repent even against unkind wind.
Fettered to the tiller of incessant approbation
Rankled the wings of one once deeply sorrowed?
Slipped away the thorn you disdain; ok, make it.

Personal Reflections

_____

_____

_____

_____

_____

Total

Have you done anything with total abandonment?
Totally, throwing yourself into a nebulous project
How about unreservedly dedicating your life to another?
Graciously forgiving abrasive encounters
Completely, disregarding your great record of rights
Close is your tenderfoot, don't miss the narrow gate.

Personal Reflections

_____

_____

_____

_____

_____

Arrival

Deep in the belly of being, there resides something.
It is beyond the effable, here the earth is filled.
Here there is nothing artificial, nothing beguiled.
There are no rash moods, treasures or fabrications.

Things eternal are conceptualized, compelling to the soul.
Tensions eased, anxiety lost and goodness expanded.
Certitude is paled by confident uncertainty.
The star leads one where wishes are no longer wishes.

That disarming moment is arriving at eternity.
Words that pierce marrow and sting joints are here.
Choruses and vibrant harps play sky-lit tunes
Set is the stage for a glorious-infinite journey.

Personal Reflections

_____

_____

_____

_____

_____

Choices

Engaged in all that activity can yield; yet life still passes by.
To dabble here or commit there or even finding middle ground
Leaving for a time, later to return; serving such little gods
Is conscience only to be remembered by self-centered prods?

It is our language that gives us well-chosen voices.
Soon to be heard, quickly to be seen we call them choices.
Revel we do in these moments fooled by impunity.
Lift this veil that shades our reason or jades our season?
Engaging what we know and relying upon our senses
We bring the past to the present and the future to the now.
The now is pervasive without thought of eternal spaces.
Yet, choices these do stand as salient in our times.
Winking out of our being, God too, demands choices.

Personal Reflections

_____

_____

_____

_____

_____

Fabulous People

Beyond the veil rises this group of humanity.
Free, full of life and letting inspiration flow
They don't make you want to love them, you do!
They live in no niches, but they live.
They prosper in a wide river of moments.
They hold you again and again, they don't relent.
Transparent, honest, true, living outside of the blue
Questions light their being, embracing solely you.
Few know their knowing, these however, are full.
Warm is their presence, reliable is their nature.
You enjoy the good fruit of their words.
No cultural abyss, they are cultured
Who seeks to engage this formative reality?
Contentment with Godliness that's their gain

Personal Reflections

_____

_____

_____

_____

_____

Purposes

A vehicle of man you know you are not
Search for truths you know not to want
Eschewing the forces of inexorable bog
Not a green toed frog on a sweated log
Purposes focus on the everlasting God.

Personal Reflections

_____

_____

_____

_____

_____

Lifting Life

No chance for offense, no place for hardness of heart.
Flail at the wind rather than be cooked in the crucible.
Countless strive for fat fixations no zest for discomfort.
Left behind are any who don't pass the common cant.
Towers, symbols, bulls and bears may chance a move?
Lay by the tracks, sniff brandy and tug at heartstrings.
If so done, the active life will be your only claim.
Going up the down staircase your quiver will be full.
Mainly of substances untouchable or rings beat thinly
Trod snowy peaks but naked remains the crux of life
You've roared quietly, you've moved only timidly.
Immune remains the soul, lusty experiences helpful?
Roams the hound of heaven, piercing your mortal coil
Now brazen and bold yet weak one can you decide?

Personal Reflections

_____

_____

_____

_____

_____

Culture

Down the court, around the diamond and passed pigskins
Lit-up is the depth or crystal thinness of current meaning.
At these adulated events even strange worship prevails.
Can culture stand? Has right language escaped us?
Frail the times, short are trusts and fleeting are loves.
Currency has wings, but many still grab the greenback.
Set aside are families, fathers and inextricable bonds.
Real culture holds no such limits its people look beyond
Ascending collides with the surety of eternal moments.
Shaping self not by the self but by the balm of Gilead
All things will pass away Alpha and Omega will remain.
There lives recreated life so dramatically inspired.
Formative and graciously persistent truth prevails.
A sage knows this, so does the plowboy and you?

Personal Reflections

_____

_____

_____

_____

_____

Clearly Woman

Wonder pierces through the steel blue eyes of this woman.
That is, it provokes wonder in the heart of the beholder.
One inquires how is it that such being has passed this way?
Unique an easy descriptor, better is joyously arcane.
Why give time to defining character or limiting glances?
Such efforts to capture this person are frail and shallow.
Instead, give heed to not knowing where she comes from.
Neither be shackled to the desperation of distant happenings.
Separate constraints and dwell quietly in an eternal moment
Now, human exchange can be fresh, stimulating and full.
That is the nature of knowing this lady of spiritual intrigue.
Hard for you but finely sweetly and facile it is for her.
You are lifted beyond what you had expected or could conceive.
Epiphany when countenance refines countenance in heavenliness.

Personal Reflections

_____

_____

_____

_____

_____

Marjeth

Vibrantly, this lady radiates freshness.
One could not say it is part of her being.
Rather, it is how she is in the world.
Sorrow and joy part; spoof a wide blush.
In those remote areas of refined thought
freshness fractures languishing stillness.
Spontaneously, joy springs to the surface.
It fans the wearied soul and revives gusto.
Joined are the ineffable and pragmatic.
When this lady sings living songs life lives.
Words weave a plaid of someone admired.
Excuse the injustice, laid I only descriptors.
A lovely frame gives her shape and texture.
God's creation is all she would claim.

Personal Reflections

_____

_____

_____

_____

_____

Hold On To

In the visible and invisible world one wonders.
Is there anything permanent to hold on to?
Economic turmoil abounds, devastating
weather and wars plague the planet.
Catastrophe then catastrophe shakes us
Fear causes some to walk as drunkards.
Deftly people try to avoid this circus of life.
The bankroll helps some back out of trouble.
Their conceit and big house insulates them.
Suddenly their only child dies - an over dose.
"How could this happen," cries their anguish.
Oddly, none of this is particularly new.
The abundance of it all distresses us.
Never leave or forsake you, says God.

Personal Reflections

_____

_____

_____

_____

_____

Avarice

Avarice is beguiling.
Corporations do it under the guise
It's an anti-business environment.
Stow another billion in the coffer.
People do it, security and power
they believe it does bring.
Bang, the bank account goes bust.
Stocks and shares mysteriously sink.
Suddenly, they are sent away empty.

Avarice looks good for a season.
It covers holes in the mortgage.
It says be something you're not.
Tomorrow you breathe your last.
Why not give profusely?
Results, a running over abundance

Personal Reflections

_____

_____

_____

_____

Leaf

Leaf falling gently,
laden with tears of dew.

Personal Reflections

_____

_____

_____

_____

Liberty

Respond, what constitutes liberty?
Is it freedom to live life free?
Free of anything of we or thee.
Free of strictures or structures.
Ideology let go, make your own ideals.
Non-consenters, let go, let be.

Utopian, this does sound.

A diamond dropped from eagle's claw.
Flawless it seems to be.
Reflections though were of me.
There I saw imperfections; yes, of me.
Cautious now I be of what I say of thee.
Not so brazen to cast a lot for another.
Purge beams in my own organs of sight.
Focus leaps upon the Jesus man.
He knew the truth of freedom right.

Personal Reflections

_____

_____

_____

_____

Darkness

Darkness assails the soul.
It is pitched against us.
Writers write in that vein.
Singers sing in that overtone.
It's painted with merit.
Achievement can write its name.
Lurking to twist your frame
Play its game, rather it plays you.
A grayed gravesite is its reward.
Only hear be the earthly domain.
Ending eternal dark beyond dismal
Lungs yet pump think again this time.
Pricked thumb sees red a flow.
Reminded deed Deity did do.

Personal Reflections

_____

_____

_____

_____

104

Oops

Oops, don't you hate that word?
It connotes something wrong.
A mistake maybe was made?
Did you frame the wrong picture?
Cut the wrong limb?
Castrated the wrong gonads!
Oops, that really had to smart.

Okay, errors played.

Non-oops needs some stay.
What could lead another way?
Wisdom beckons this day.
Plied by prejudice it splinters along the way.
Implemented by oops, not so gay.
Light, intensely more light, there stay.

Personal Reflections

_____

_____

_____

_____

Her

Inside this lady are cries for love, her heart speaks
and leaves behind ineffable chagrin.
To touch the gentleness of her thoughts stirs one
with sweet intrigue and an enlarged life.
Humor easily from her frame and with it she
softens the skin of calloused people.
So easy then is it to share of life with her, it makes
the chat honest, clean and engaging.
All, thankfully cannot be said of her, for she still has
those shades that cover quietude.
In those impenetrable places ride some insecurities,
uncertainties and confusing issues.
Don't we all have them? Yet, they govern not her behavior
nor distort her countenance.
So, why not stand next to her and take some time
to hear the story of this radiant life?
For in her is some of you, some of me and most
impressively some of glorious eternity.
Not only limited to those who stand without affliction
she has bowed her knee with death.
As the last breath of human existence has slipped
past wrinkled lips she has comforted
and heard these words "one more hug from mom,
daddy please don't die or son...son."
Vagaries of life and time have then come close to
her broadly-limited in depth journey.
Now and for infinity she presses on with Jesus within
and heart bent on the loving God.

Sauna

There's better theology in a sauna
than in divinity schools.
In divinity schools God is esoteric,
Greek, laden with titles, and distant.
That is, he's out there somewhere.

In a sauna the hand of God is clearly seen
as black, brown, yellow, red or white.
Men talk of job loss, lies, not returning
evil for evil, deception, women, work,
a clear conscience and the bite of life.
The force of honesty in their words
makes them hang on to you.
In fact, you want them to, stuck on
changing your ground pounding.
When finished, you know God
has been in your midst.
When you finish divinity school a lot
of textbooks are thrown into the river.

Turn up the steam, come
sweat for a while.

Personal Reflections

The Author

Ted has been writing poetry for many decades. Admittedly, it has not been a consistent, timely process. Rather, it has come in spurts, sputters, bumps and grinds. Trusting that most of what he has written has been "inspired from on high," much of it has flowed effortlessly. Other times he has beat the air for words. This is, probably, not too dissimilar from colleagues who have attempted to put poetic phrasing on paper.

His themes cover a bevy of issues. The point is to hit upon topics or ideas to which most people can embrace. In so doing, there will be common ground for discussion, public reading or quiet pensive moments. Latitude is given to the reader to both feel the impact, and formulate thoughts concerning each piece. It is hoped that the outcome would always be uplifting, enjoyable and, in some cases, personally challenging.

If you come across Ted sitting in a coffee shop with a timeless gaze upon his face, its dollars to donuts he has just hit upon a new idea for a sonnet. If such is not the case, he's pondering a creative move for an Argentine Tango!